Cracking Bitcoin

Max Taylor

Max Taylor

Copyright © 2018 Max Taylor

All rights reserved.

ISBN-13: 9781981000715

CRACKING BITCOIN

CONTENTS

Intro to Cracking   8

Cracking Basics   15

Cracking Trading   27

Cracking Investing   54

Cracking Mining and Proof of Stake   77

Closing   101

CRACKING BITCOIN

Max Taylor

CRACKING BITCOIN

Chapter 1
Intro to Cracking

Everyone always wants to be the first to find out what the next big thing is. No doubt even Bitcoin's biggest detractors secretly wish they could go back and buy a bunch of Bitcoin at a dollar and be a multi-millionaire by now. Unfortunately, as much as I love that 80's DeLorean, we still can't time travel yet.

The fact remains, however, that we are still in the early stages of crypto adoption. There are so many things to be excited about in the future. I cannot stress enough how much opportunity there is inside the crypto world. The blockchain technology that underlies cryptocurrency will almost certainly become a significant part of our everyday lives in ways most of us haven't even imagined yet.

As with any significant technological advancement in society, there comes a fantastic opportunity to capitalize on the technology and utilize different pieces of it to generate large quantities of income and wealth. You must simply just look at the Industrial Revolution, the Internet Revolution, etc. Industry insiders all agree this groundswell has tremendous potential to be just as monumental. I'm not one to continually exaggerate, and you'll see I can be brutally honest when needed throughout the book. That said, I do not believe I can overstate the amount of opportunity that lies ahead in this world.

Even with this entire book, I can only touch the tips of each subject's iceberg. Does this deep, dark world of cryptocurrency scare you a bit? These traits are actually precisely what you should want to see. Complexity breeds opportunity. We do not want something too easy. Take early Bitcoin adopters, for instance. Oh sure, on the surface it may look like the people that bought Bitcoin at $1.00 in 2011 and held (that is an EXTREMELY tiny number of individuals by the way) made easy money. The facts are, though, that these select few so-called "lucky" individuals understood extremely early how powerful Bitcoin could be.

Why did they believe in it, though? Simple… because they were some of the first to understand the needs it addressed and how it could revolutionize the world of finance and technology. Most people had not even heard of Bitcoin, much less done in-depth research on it. Not only did these "lucky" people understand something that very few did, but they also had massive amounts of discipline that allowed them to ride an incredible roller coaster to get to where we are today. These people didn't get rich quick. They got rich in a disciplined, intelligent manner. You see, when something is so easy that anyone can do it, then that thing loses its intrinsic value as a money-making tool. If you're reading this book you're part of a small percentage of the population that's willing to put their mind where their mouth is.

Bitcoin and all her cryptocurrency siblings have been all the rage in the media for the past couple of years. In the world I live in, though, crypto went viral a long time ago. Crypto is so much more than some get rich quick scheme. Crypto and its underlying technology, the blockchain, has the potential to change the world in the same way that the internet has altered every day of our life. It will not only change the way we spend money but potentially the way we hold real estate, the way governments secure nuclear codes, and even the manner in which we conduct ourselves on the World Wide Web. It is this world-changing potential that has given cryptocurrency and blockchain tech the fuel to become the incredible force that it is today. From a financial standpoint, history has shown us that if you get involved heavily in something that alters the way we live our daily lives, there are enormous amounts of profits to be made. Cryptocurrency is one of those rare opportunities that affords you the benefit of doing good for society and for your pocketbook all at the same time.

If you listen to the major media outlets, the talk has centered merely around Bitcoin as a speculative investment or currency. While there is most certainly plenty to be said of cryptocurrency as an investment, what the media outlets fail to convey to the public is how many genuinely diverse opportunities there are within the cryptocurrency world. The media has a very narrow view and knowledge of the crypto world. Never forget that fact when you are scrolling through the news and read some "financial expert's" opinion that a particular crypto is worthless. People hate what they don't understand, and the mainstream media undoubtedly does not understand this market.

If there is one thing we have found out about Bitcoin and

cryptocurrency in 2017-2018, it is that the "crypto coaster" can be one heck of a ride. So how can we mitigate the highs and lows of the insanity? That is no easy task, but it can be accomplished with discipline and knowledge. My primary goal throughout this book is to provide you with a set of tools that you can start with and expand from. This book is not a comprehensive guide, yet it is packed with extremely useful information.

If you get anything at all out of this book get this: money can be made in cryptocurrency in a multitude of ways. It can be made in an up-market, in a stagnant market, and in a down-market. Everyone wants to know when and if Bitcoin is here forever or just a while. The point I want to get across is that it doesn't matter. There is money waiting to be made by someone with the willingness to research, learn and dive in.

In my opinion, the smartest thing to do is get involved with crypto in multiple ways. So, get deep into this book, take a couple that sound interesting to you, and move your learning to a whole new level. I wrote this book to give you a detailed introduction to the many different income streams that cryptocurrency provides. It is not meant to make you an expert in each one of them. That would take a book longer than any of us are probably up for. Your job, then, is to decide which avenues to chase wholly. Then, go out there, full force, and make it happen. Making money with crypto is not just the opportunity of 2018. It could be the opportunity of a lifetime if you're willing to put in the work and dedicate yourself to learning and advancement.

Don't be afraid to jump around in this book. If some subject matter strikes you as dull as a community college class on underwater basket weaving, then do the author and yourself a favor... SKIP IT!!! You can always come back to it later if you feel it necessary. Find at least two, maybe three concepts in the book that really get your blood pumping. Focus on those and become proficient in them. Remember this: knowledge plus passion equals purposed success.

I want to be very, very clear... I am not a financial advisor, nor should you follow mine or anyone else's (including a financial advisor's) advice without doing plenty of your own research. As I have heard before, "trust but verify."

Now, let's rock and roll!

CHAPTER 2
CRACKING BASICS

Before we get chest deep into making money, I want to quickly cover some necessary basics of the technology and terminology behind crypto. Knowing these will give us a platform on which to build on in the following chapters. To start this foundation, let's look at the foundation of all cryptos: the blockchain.

Blockchain Technology

As with many other things in this book, an entire volume couldn't contain the details of blockchain technology and all of its intricacies. What I am aiming for here, though, is to give a simple description that will allow you to understand the principles behind it. A good, technical definition of blockchain is a "transparent, public, append-only ledger." Clear as mud, right? Let's dive in a bit to the ins and outs of the blockchain, and maybe that definition will make more sense to you shortly.

Blockchains are primarily being used to fill a hole that the internet has never truly been able to fill. While the internet has allowed a massive transfer of knowledge across the world, one thing it has never been able to do efficiently is to allow a safe transfer of monetary value. Companies such as PayPal have made some advances in addressing this problem; however, you are still going to an institution or a bank to send that money from point A to point B. When being used with crypto assets, blockchain allows money to be sent directly from one source to another without a middleman.

At its core, a blockchain is a distributed database that records a series of digital events or transactions that occur across a network. This distributed database underlies the network and enables tracking a transaction of value. The recording of a transaction or event registry is referred to as the "ledger." Multiple independent sources will verify each transaction that takes place within that ledger.

Think of the ledger as a balanced checkbook. For those of

you who have ever balanced a checkbook (which may genuinely be a small percentage of readers in this day and age), all transactions, whether deposits or withdrawals, that take place within your bank account are recorded within the checkbook. Once all transactions are recorded for that specific period, you simply take the balance at the beginning of that timeframe and go line by line subtracting the withdrawals and adding the deposits. The balance at the end of the time period should match your current balance in your account. What the ledger does is allow this verified "balancing of the checkbook" after each transaction takes place. So, if person "A" wishes to send crypto to person "B," the independent verifiers would look at the ledger to see that person "A" has the specified amount of crypto before verifying that transaction for person "B."

The blockchain is a system for creating consensus between scattered or distributed parties that do not need to trust each other. When I send or receive a determined value of cryptocurrency, I don't place trust in a centralized person or company such as a bank. I trust the mechanism by which the consensus was reached. I trust the blockchain.

From a security standpoint, blockchains rely on a form of randomized challenges so that no single entity on the network can consistently solve this challenge more than everyone else. No one verifier can force the blockchain to accept a particular entry onto the ledger that others disagree with. The blockchain is built on a peer-to-peer network that can maintain updates to the ledger and then verify those updates in such a way that it is impossible to defraud and impossible to alter after the fact. We will speak more about the verification process in later chapters.

Terms to Know

There are several terms in the "crypto world" that it would serve you well to know. Some of these terms will be used throughout the book as well. Feel free to bookmark these terms and return to them as you run into the terms you don't understand.

Cryptocurrency Exchange: A marketplace for the buying, selling, and trading of cryptocurrencies and assets.

Blockchain: A transparent, public, append-only ledger that verifies ledger entries using consensus

Distributed Ledger: A database held and updated by a large number of self-determining participants in a network.

HODL: A crypto-specific term that refers to holding an investment through volatility in the hopes that its value grows exponentially.

Fiat Currency: Legal tender as determined by a governing body that is not backed by any physical commodity such as gold.

Altcoins: Initially a term used to refer to all cryptocurrencies and crypto assets other than Bitcoin. More recently evolved into referring to cryptos outside the top 3-5 market cap cryptos (those much less well known to the public).

Cryptocurrencies vs. Crypto assets

In the mainstream media, you will hear just two words used when talking about all things crypto: "Bitcoin" or "cryptocurrency." Now that you are looking to further your education, you need to understand that all cryptos are unquestionably not created equal. Merriam-Webster Dictionary defines a currency as "something (such as coins, treasury notes, and banknotes) that is in circulation as a medium of exchange." Due to current limitations, very few cryptos are true currencies. They lack widespread adoption across marketplaces and really are only tradeable for other cryptos or fiat currency. However, if the crypto's primary function and purpose are to become a literal form of money or exchange of value, then it should still be classified as a cryptocurrency.

What many people don't realize is that a clear majority of cryptos are not in any way meant to be currencies. Many are never intended to purchase something but, instead, have a wide variety of other functions. For all these non-currency cryptos, a more appropriate term is "crypto asset." As we dive more into the investing side of crypto, we will go over some differences in crypto assets such as utility vs. security assets. Moving forward, when I use the term "crypto," I am collectively grouping currencies and assets.

"Coins" vs. "Tokens"

Much as with the "cryptocurrency" term, you may hear all crypto units referred to as coins but there are crypto coins and crypto tokens. The two differ greatly from one another. A crypto "coin" is something that functions primarily as a currency or store of value. Examples of this include Bitcoin and Litecoin. Crypto "tokens" are significantly different in the sense that they are based on technology built on a platform such as Ethereum. Tokens are programmable and can store a complex array of functions. Generally speaking, tokens have some utility that ties to the project behind the coin.

ICOs and TGEs

ICOs (Initial Coin Offerings) and TGEs (Token Generation Events) are announced and pre-planned times for new crypto projects to offer a set number of tokens or coins to early adopters. Generally speaking, an ICO or TGE will offer their crypto units for a fixed price which you can pay for using another dominant cryptocurrency or asset. Once payment is made, the new coins or tokens purchased are sent to a compatible wallet that you have previously set up.

An ICO or TGE will almost always take place before the project is fully completed or, in some cases, before it has even started. The funds raised are used to move the project forward and cover operating expenses. It is very similar to a "crowdfunding" system. As with anything, where the money goes to something with only the promise of what is coming and nothing to truly back it up, there is a high risk / high reward element to it. Obviously, there have been some bad actor ICOs in the past, and there will be more in the future. Background research is vital when evaluating an ICO or TGE.

ICOs and TGEs can also work as an initial distribution model that will provide liquidity when exchanges start adding the coins or tokens for trade.

Exchanges

Much as a US stock market trader executes trades using the New York Stock Exchange or NASDAQ, crypto has a variety of exchanges from where to buy, sell and trade cryptocurrency. Most readers have likely heard of Coinbase which is the largest U.S. based exchange. Multiple other large exchanges are physically based all over the world.

Choosing good exchanges is one of the most critical choices you'll make early on in your crypto journey. I would recommend starting out with one of the more significant, more well-known exchanges. After getting the hang of that, move on to accounts at other trustworthy exchanges. Having accounts at multiple large exchanges will allow you to diversify your money, enjoy different benefits and have access to a broader number of cryptos. Understand that not all exchanges have a "fiat gate" or a way to deposit USD, EURO, etc. To get liquidity onto these exchanges, you will have to deposit via crypto. Moving crypto from one exchange to another is usually relatively straightforward. Certain cryptos naturally take longer than others to get from point A to point B. We are still in the new stages of this crypto revolution. Occasionally, exchange websites will go down, or the ability to trade will become extremely slow. Understand that we are part of a massive growth stage. Having two to three exchanges that you use on a regular basis will allow you to shift from one site to the other.

As we already touched on, there are a plethora of options when it comes to choosing an exchange. Some are well-established giants while some are up and coming. You'll also see several exchanges that have been around for a good while that seem to attract a small, dedicated following. There are several things you want to look at before you choose an exchange. Appearances and popularity can be deceiving.

Most importantly, look at the reputation of the exchange. As with online reviews of any kind, negativity is always going to be overrepresented. The anger is exaggerated even further because these exchanges are dealing with people's money. You will have to look at several forums and review boards to entirely get an idea of whether or not there are real issues. Use your judgment as a filter to weed out the vitriol and get down to the facts.

Begin by looking for one that is not regularly down with server issues. Keep in mind that every exchange will have some server issues as crypto has indeed gone viral. You just don't want one that is regularly down as it is likely at the peak traffic times that some of the best trading opportunities will arise. Many exchanges will even restrict new user registration for short periods of time if they feel their servers have reached their capacity. You may see negativity about an exchange doing that. In my view, that is an excellent sign that they are more concerned about the quality of service than the quantity of customers.

One of the main negative trends to watch out for are repeated issues and delays with withdrawals and deposits. A poorly run exchange will often have problems that they fail to resolve for several days or even weeks on end. As a trader, if your funds are suspended somewhere in cyberspace in between exchanges, you could end up losing a significant percentage due to missed opportunity or the inability to get out at the top of a downward slide. Don't look for isolated incidents as it could always be user error. Instead, look for a pattern of failures and issues.

I would also always look to see if an exchange has had any security issues in the past and how they have resolved those issues. For example, if an exchange has been attacked and recovered from that attack while restoring lost funds, that says a significant amount about their trustworthiness. Also, if a massive exchange has not had significant security issues, that is unquestionably good; however, it certainly doesn't guarantee future security. Always diversify yourself. Never put all your "eggs" in one exchange "basket."

Finally, I know most readers won't do this, but I highly recommend you literally sit down and read the terms and conditions of the exchange for which you are signing up. I know, I know... what a bore! We are talking about your money, though, and, hopefully, large amounts of it as you grow your portfolio. These decisions are paramount and should be treated as such.

Wallets

There is a difference between a crypto wallet and a crypto exchange. A crypto wallet is simply a place to store your cryptocurrency and crypto assets. While every exchange has wallets as a necessity (there must be a place to store cryptos when trading is not occurring), there are many stand-alone wallets available.

Both online and offline crypto wallets exist for storing crypto long term. Offline wallets or "cold storage" wallets are considered the most secure in the sense that they cannot be forcibly hacked due to their lack of connection. Both online and offline wallets have a public wallet address and a private wallet "key." The private key is what is needed for you to withdraw or send funds.

PRO TIP: Never, ever provide your wallet private key to someone. That key will allow them full access to your funds and would make it possible to withdraw those funds in an unrecoverable manner. Also, just as important, place your secret key in a disconnected (not online), extremely secure place. If you misplace, lose or destroy this key, you will be completely unable to access your funds. For security purposes, there is no "recover password" type of option.

As your crypto wealth increases, I would highly recommend you investigate storing a large chunk of your crypto in an offline wallet. It is always better to diversify so don't put everything in one wallet, especially if it's a significant enough amount.

Chapter 3
Cracking Trading

For this book, I have separated trading and investing into two entirely different revenue streams. Those familiar with traditional forms of investment and trading may already understand some of the differences. That being said, in cryptocurrency, the differences are even more pronounced due to the constant high level of volatility. Traders and investors may play on the same playground, but they are very different species. Both are truly necessary for the market to operate smoothly.

Cryptocurrency investors are most concerned with the potential and eventual value of a particular coin. Traders, on the other hand, are much more concerned with the current state of the marketplace and the short-term future of specific coins. Though there are many different investment strategies in crypto, all true investments are meant to make money over an extended period of time. Conversely, cryptocurrency trading revolves around frequently buying and selling. The goal, of course, is to outperform the market consistently. To oversimplify it: "buy low sell high" as many times as you possibly can. Ah… if only it was that easy.

I will begin this section by explaining some basic concepts you need as a foundation then we are going to get into some specific trading strategies.

Understanding the Exchange

At this point, I would highly suggest if you haven't already signed up for an exchange or two, take the time to get that done. As you read through some of the explanations below, it will be much less confusing if you're looking at what I am explaining. It isn't all that complex, but it can sometimes sound and look that way. Once you get it down, it is just common sense. So grab yourself an energy drink or a cup of coffee, swing by the resource website, pick a couple of exchanges and run through the sign-up process. Before you deposit money, though, you really should research the exchange some yourself.

Don't just take my opinion about an exchange and run with it. I am sure every exchange will have issues. Our suggested ones are no exception. As with everything in this book, do your research. I am not a financial advisor. I am not investing your money. You are. Do your own research. Understand the risks. Then move forward with confidence.

Now, let's talk about some things you will see on your exchange and what they mean.

Once you get into your main Exchange trading page, there will be choices consisting of Fiat/Crypto (such as US Dollar to Bitcoin) exchanges or Crypto/Crypto (such as Bitcoin to Ethereum) exchanges. At first, it will look like a foreign language if you're unfamiliar with crypto trading. Fear not, though. It will be easier to understand than you think. Each "currency," whether Fiat or crypto, will have its own dedicated ticker symbol on each exchange. For instance, the US Dollar would be USD. Bitcoin would be BTC. Be sure to research each of the ticker symbols on your chosen exchange(s) as they may differ between exchanges.

Once you find the currency pair you wish to view, click on it to go to the currency trading page. On the currency pair trading page, you will typically see a set of green numbers and a set of red numbers. This is referred to as the order book. The red numbers indicate selling bids and the green numbers indicate buy bids. Think of it this way. All trades are made up of at least two orders. One order for the buyer and one order for the seller. The seller will have to agree to the buyer's price, or the buyer will have to agree to the seller's price. Thanks to the impersonal nature of the internet, this is all done without you even thinking about it too much.

Order Types

The two most common ways to place a buy or sell order on exchanges are market orders or limit orders. Limit orders are placed when a buyer or seller wishes to dictate a specific price at which they are willing to buy or sell. If a limit order is matched by another buyer/seller, then the order will be filled. It will simply sit there until either canceled or matched and filled. Market orders are placed when the seller or buyer is willing to purchase at whatever the market price may be. In other words, if you place a market order, you will buy/sell at what the limit order sellers/buyers are asking.

The third type of order option that your chosen exchange may include is called a stop order. Stop orders come in a few different forms such as stop-limit or stop-loss. In general, stop orders are designed to trigger a sell or buy if a price drops or rises to a certain point. This can help give you peace of mind if you must step away from the desk for a little while or even if you want to leave funds in a volatile crypto overnight. It is designed to help stop a loss or solidify a win. For instance, if you purchased a certain crypto in the morning at $100 USD and the price is equal to $120 USD by bedtime, you may not want to sell. You may feel that the uptrend will continue and that it may be worth $140 by the next morning. At the same time, you don't want to lose all the profit that you've gained if it drops back down to $100. In this scenario, you may wish to set a stop order to sell at market price if the price drops down to, say, $110. This would still ensure a very respectable return on investment while still allowing you the opportunity to make even more.

Charts and How to Read Them

Now that you have a basic understanding of the numbers

you're seeing, you are probably asking yourself what the heck all these charts. If you know what you're looking at, charts and graphs can be some of the most valuable information you have.

The first and most simple chart you will see on some exchanges is the line chart. This chart is very self-explanatory and simply shows the progression over time. Some exchanges will include line charts showing such things as volume and market share in addition to the standard price progression line graph.

For a more advanced view, a candlestick chart can show you more detail within a certain trading period. A candlestick chart is a lineup of vertical bars that indicate price changes across a certain time frame. Each vertical bar is either red or green with a thin line extending from the bar's top, bottom or both. Each of these "candlesticks," as they are called, represents a certain period of time. The amount of time each candle represents can be adjusted from days all the way down to minutes. The candle represents four price points within its time frame. The thick bar represents the opening price and the closing price. The thin line, called the wick, indicates the highest-reached price and the lowest-reached price within that time period.

On the candlestick chart, you will see both green and red candlesticks. The green ones are gaining, "bullish" candlesticks that indicate positive price movement. With the bullish candlestick, the top part of the main candle indicates the closing price of that time frame. The bottom of the bullish candle represents the starting or open price of that time period. A red candlestick is the opposite of the above and bearish candle's top represents the open, and the bottom represents the close.

The final chart you will see on most exchanges is the depth chart. The depth chart is a visual representation of the current limit orders that are unfilled and outstanding. Buy orders will generally be green and on the left of the chart. Conversely, sell orders will generally be red and on the right. The horizontal axis at the bottom of the chart represents each price point that the limit orders are placed at. The vertical axis along the sides of the chart represents the total value of orders at that price point.

Now, if none of that chart crap makes a bit of sense to you,

you aren't alone, I'm sure. Just get familiar with the exchange, and you can come back to the above discussion with much more understanding.

Charts provide traders with information that can help them loosely predict upcoming swings based on trends from the past indicators. Though they are great indicators, even Nostradamus couldn't predict crypto futures. I could go on for an entire chapter on ways to read and use the information on these graphs. As I said at the beginning of the book, once you choose which route to go down, it will be vital for you to continue your learning. Remember, knowledge is power.

Volume and Market Cap

The volume and market cap of a crypto are two of the most important factors to look at when considering trading it. Both of these can easily be found on coinmarketcap.com or a similar site. So, what do these mean and why are they so important?

A crypto's volume tells how much it has done in sales in a past time frame, usually a 24-hour day. Volume can indicate a crypto's ability to be sold or moved quickly. This can be critical information for a crypto trader who is trading in and out throughout the day. If a trader were to purchase a crypto at an apparent great price but is unable to sell it when the time is right, it is not a successful trade but merely a successful buy. Since trading does not involve long-term holding, you must always look for the ability to exit quickly when your desired profit is made.

When looking at a crypto's overall volume, be sure to look at your specific exchange's volume as well. In certain scenarios, one particular exchange may hold the bulk of a crypto's volume and your exchange hold too small of a percentage.

PRO TIP: As you become an advanced trader, you will regularly follow some certain cryptos of your choosing. You will be monitoring price, news, etc. You will also want to monitor volume. Many times (not always) a steep volume increase will be a precursor to a significant price shift. In can help you decide to get in or out of a crypto before the shift. Prediction is a superpower in trading and the more tools you have in your prediction tool belt, the better.

Market share can sometimes show a lot more than price.

Remember, just because a coin is selling for a very low price doesn't necessarily mean that its market cap is low. If there are 1 billion coins in circulation, even a $0.02 coin can have a strong market cap. Many people fail to realize that a crypto's "circulating supply" can be deceiving. For instance, there may be large quantities of initial coin or token rewards given to early investors and founders that have been off exchanges since their inception. Also, certain cryptos have large percentages that have been lost by their users. Some experts estimate that around 10% of the circulating supply of Bitcoin has been lost. Most of that loss is by users who did not value it in its earliest days. One way to see how legitimate a crypto's market cap is you can look at the total trading volume on exchanges. A lack of liquidity on exchanges means something is a bit fishy. As a general rule, a healthy crypto will generally average a daily trading volume between 5% and 10% of its total dollar market cap.

Margin Trading

One of the things you're going to see on many of the exchange sites is an option to do what is called margin trading. Margin trading can be a beneficial tool but can also be very,

very dangerous for a new or somewhat unseasoned trader. There are different kinds of margin trading, but the main concept you need to grasp is that it is borrowing money to trade on that Exchange. Of course, there is an interest rate involved in margin trading. Either the crypto you are borrowing comes from other users on the exchange that have chosen to lend out their crypto, or it comes directly from the exchange. Your initial stake is what provides collateral for the lender. Use of this leverage can undoubtedly magnify your profits in, but the reverse is also true. A trader could be hit with massive losses or even lose their entire initial investment. Again, great risk and great potential reward.

One of the most powerful things about crypto is how decentralized it is. That being said, one potential downside of this decentralization is the lack of protection. The decentralized model does put a lot of responsibility on the back of every individual who gets involved in it. One example is the lack of agencies regulating how much you can borrow or how much you owe in margin trading. Be extremely careful not to dig yourself into a hole that you can't get out of. There's no one keeping you from digging your own grave. Big brother is not watching over you. If you're like me, you wouldn't want Big

Brother watching over you anyway. Just make sure you have the knowledge and the discipline to protect yourself. Margin trading, as with any form of borrowing, can be a great tool in the financial world but it can also be the end of you.

PRO TIP: You should also have a deep understanding of fees on each exchange as this could make or break a trade. You may make half a percent on the trade but then lose it all in fees. Know the cost of doing business before you jump in head-first.

Futures Trading

For those who are unfamiliar, a futures contract is a contract to purchase or sell an asset or commodity at both a stated, specific price and at a future, predetermined time. On crypto exchanges that allow it, it is generally inside the world of margin trading is where you find futures and the ability to either take either a short or a long position on a cryptocurrency.

If your target crypto was trading at $2,000 per coin or token and you believe it will be coming back down soon, you may take a short on it for $1,900, betting that in a set period of time the price would drop to $1,900 or below. If you took a long position on it, you take the position at $2,100. Understanding options trading within ANY asset environment is extremely dangerous and volatile. Multiply that by the natural volatility of crypto, and you have something that could make you millions or lose you everything you have… in some cases, overnight. When dabbling in options, be informed, be careful and be prepared for whatever outcome may occur. Never risk more than you can lose.

PRO TIP: Recently many large financial institutions and exchanges such as the Chicago Mercantile Exchange (CME) began to allow the trading of futures on Bitcoin. Remember, this is entirely outside of the type of exchanges we are dealing with. In truth, these agencies usually aren't even trading Bitcoin. There is no purchase a Bitcoin or sale of Bitcoin only a transaction based on the price of Bitcoin and what it is now compared to what it will be in the future. This is a very standard operating procedure within the stock market and other investment environments.

Algorithmic Trading

Algorithmic trading has been part of trading within professional exchanges of all kinds for years. It only makes sense that in a world initially dominated by programmers, geeks and gamers, that algorithmic trading would hold even more significant influence in crypto trading. The more trading you do, the more you will learn to recognize when you are competing against a bot or a trading algorithm. Algorithmic trading uses computer programmed bots that are connected via API (Application Programming Interface) to each exchange to make lightning-fast trades. Many bots can enter or remove bids in mere milliseconds, making it very tough to compete against them in a bidding war that takes place with limit bids. You may place the highest buy bid only to be outbid in less than a second later by .000001 Bitcoin. This can be incredibly frustrating unless you are the one that is using the bot. With time, you will learn how to use someone else's bot either against them or for you. This will make the existence of these bots much more endurable, I assure you.

If you wish to enter the complex world of algorithms and bots yourself, there are opportunities to do so. An algorithmic trading bot can be set up using predefined indicators that tell the bot when to buy when to sell and at what price. Advanced bots can use machine learning and historical data to improve performance. Bots can be programmed by a programmer you hire or, if you have enough technical knowledge, you could program it yourself. You can also find some open source options and ones for sale on GitHub.com. If you don't want to go through the trouble of building your own or having one built, there are marketplaces for rental algorithms as well as subscription-based companies that offer all-in-one solutions. These marketplace or ready-to-use algorithms can be easy to implement and potentially even profitable. Keep in mind, though, if a developer creates a highly profitable bot, why would he or she sell that bot? For that reason, most of the bots that you will find for sale or rent online are likely only moderately profitable if at all. There are, however, a few good bots out there.

Building a trading algorithm for yourself or having one built for you is a highly advanced strategy if you want to be truly successful at it. If you genuinely want to have a highly profitable bot, you will first need to understand the strategy that you want that bot to implement. You must find a successful strategy before you look to have an algorithm written for you. Trading strategies across markets can sometimes work regardless of the commodity. There is a significant amount of information out there concerning algorithmic trading in centralized marketplaces such as the New York Stock Exchange. You can take this info and consider whether it would apply in the crypto trading world. The number of strategies that exist is practically endless. Obviously, you need to focus on ones that work well in highly volatile markets due to the volatility of crypto. Find some strategies that you believe have potential and learn to understand them. If possible, once you get a grasp on the strategy, try it out in regular trading and prove it before you have an algorithm built on the back of the theory.

One of the main tools you will need to use when looking at a trading algorithm is called backtesting. You should always backtest whether you are renting, buying or you had an algorithm built. Backtesting will take a defined time and look at trading history to see if the parameters of your algorithm would have proved profitable during that time frame. If your algorithm is reliable, you will see multiple examples of it working during separate time periods. When looking to rent or buy an algorithm, never trust an algorithm's writer or seller to do the back testing for you. They may publish examples of backtested periods, but you need to do your own backtesting. For all you know they are showing a time frame that was very favorable to the algorithm as opposed to a random time frame. There are websites that you can use to back test your own algorithms. For algorithms bought or rented, you will generally find backtesting availability inside their Marketplace. For algorithms that you either write or have written, you would have to do your own backtesting using programs you create or ones that you find in places such as GitHub.

PRO TIP: Learn the basics of day trading manually before you try to make an automated strategy that could lose all of your money in a matter of minutes If programmed incorrectly. If I sound like an alarmist, it may be because I've made enough mistakes to learn the hard way. It is indeed exciting to think about income automation aided by computers. Don't get caught up in all the hype without having the knowledge to back it up though. That is just a recipe for disaster.

The 4 Pillars

From my own experience and the shared experience of others throughout the crypto community, I have put together four key elements that every crypto trader should strive to master. I am referring to these as the four pillars of crypto trading... partially because it sounds catchy... but, more importantly, because the combination of these four traits will truly support profitable trading.

Pillar #1: Technical Analysis. Making decisions based on technical analysis is one of the most popular strategies used by successful crypto traders today. Technical analysis uses charts of price movement and various other analytical tools to uncover trends and predict future price changes. At its core, technical analysis is the study of the forces of supply and demand. These forces are directly reflected in the price movement. Tracking the relation of the supply or demand to such things as the price movement and trading volume can lead you to the ability to predict future movement. As with everything, understanding and ability come from study and experience. As with anything in the crypto world, it is hard to predict. Nevertheless, if you learn from history, then you can certainly greatly increase your chance of success.

Some traders rely too heavily on trends and say to ignore everything else and only believe the charts. They believe the data, not the sentiment, rumors, and news. Although this has some solid reasoning on the surface, the one thing you must remember is that, while all markets can be driven by emotion, no market can be driven more by emotion than the cryptocurrency market. This is especially true with the massive influx of new investors that have flooded the marketplace. Remember that if bad news catches hold, there could be a short-term panic sell of certain cryptos. I believe you should at least keep your finger on the pulse of what's going on in the public eye. You can believe the charts a majority of the time, but be aware when something irregular occurs in the marketplace.

Pillar #2: Intuition. In many ways, directly opposite of the technical analysis sits the skill of intuition. Intuition, to put it simply, is trusting your gut. In the institutional world of trading, intuitive traitors don't get a lot of respect; however, in the universe of crypto, many of the most highly respected traders and investors made their fortunes with some form of intuitive trading/investing. After all, there was only so much information available four years ago concerning cryptocurrency. Many of the early adopters simply trusted their gut more than anything.

Please understand that utilizing intuition does not mean you are uninformed. In today's crypto markets the most successful intuitive traders are the ones with the most experience. Studies have shown that what we call "gut instinct" is usually just our mind processing all of the information it receives through the filters of past experience. So, don't just expect yourself to have the golden finger every time you click your mouse to trade. Just because you think you know something is going to go well, doesn't mean you have the experience to back up that gut instinct. Many new traders will be unprofitable at the beginning if they are making emotionally charged decisions as opposed to decisions based on past experience and knowledge. Developing a knowledge-backed intuition will take time. Don't even try to use it at first. That being said, once you do have the experience to back it up against, be sure to trust that gut instinct. It can lead you down some very profitable paths in trading.

Pillar #3: Information. In my opinion, anyone aspiring to be a successful trader should fully immerse themselves in knowing and understanding the market and its offerings. A truly informed crypto trader spends part of virtually every day sifting through the latest forums and news. Staying informed can include using tools such as Google Trends to understand if new crypto has had a spike in interest. Websites like steemit.com, bitcointalk.org, cryptocurrencytalk.com or, of course, good ole reddit.com can provide a wealth of insider knowledge. I would highly suggest you follow crypto experts and companies on Twitter and Telegram. Their insights can help significantly shorten your learning curve as well as keep you informed. You should work every day to stay on the cutting edge of technological advancements, coin partnerships, press or anything else that might cause the general investing and trading public to boost a certain coin. If you can get even a slight head start, it can make all the difference between small gains and massive ones.

Pillar #4: Sentiment. Every market is driven by people, and the majority of people are driven by emotion. It stands to reason, then, that market sentiment does not always align with an asset's true value. As you dive into crypto, you will see countless examples of illogical rises and falls that have no fundamental reasoning whatsoever. You may see some spectacular partnership announced around a certain crypto and think, rightfully so, that its value should shoot up. While many times it will, you will be frustrated to find that many times it won't and sometimes it will even go down. What is the reason behind this? Simple… There is no reason. It is emotion, not reason that is driving pricing.

Sentiment has always been a part of institutional investing with many stocks going up and down based on the fear or excitement factor. More than any other market though, the crypto markets move up and down solely based on sentiment many times. Sentiment played a key part in the massive growth of crypto markets in 2017. Most new crypto investors during a boom have no clue what they are getting into. They just know they want to ride a train to riches. "FOMO" or "fear of missing out" is the most common emotional change agent in the crypto market. If a crypto starts going up, people want to jump on the train. Once it gets high enough, people want to take their profits. They fear that if they don't sell NOW, they may lose some or all of what they gained. The reverse is true for a crypto moving downward. The "get out while you can" mentality has turned many a crypto's 5% loss into a 25% or more loss.

The good news is, more than any time in human history, public sentiment can be measured by everything from forums to what's trending on social media. While you may not see things unfold before your eyes on Reddit or Twitter, these channels will give you insight into how the general public thinks. Uninformed traders can significantly affect pricing in a market like we see today in cryptocurrency. This means a smart, informed trader must not only think like a smart trader but also be able to understand the sentiments of an uninformed trader. The combination of these two skills can be very hard to master but can be an absolute money grabber in the world of crypto trading.

Now that I have shared these 4 pillars with you, I want you to understand that there is not any perfect combination. Each individual trader will utilize one or two of the pillars more than others. That is definitely ok. You should always focus on your strengths, but you should be working in the background to beef up those weaknesses too. Never stop improving and bettering yourself. Life inside or outside the crypto world can be lived more fully if you never settle for average.

PRO TIP: Remember that there is no such thing as a foolproof trading strategy. Every strategy has things that can go wrong. Some are higher risk levels than others. Remember to find a proper balance of risk and reward based on what you see an acceptable and what your goals are with trading.

Exit Strategy Discipline

If you master everything we have spoken about so far and trade like a boss, but you miss what we are about to talk about, you can kiss your profits goodbye. Now that I have your attention, let's talk exit strategy discipline. How could your exit strategy be so important you ask? With a market as volatile as crypto, your exit strategy must be a hard and fast rule. You can end up losing profit or extending losses in a massive way.

Every trade you enter should have a point and purpose. There should be a reason why you're making the trade. So many amateur traders jump in and out of trades with no thought. Of course, even a blind squirrel finds a nut every once in a while, but the more you do this the more likely you are to lose the bulk of your initial investment. Using the skills outlined thus far, you have to develop strategies and reasonings on why to get into certain assets. From there, you formulate a strategy to exit each asset or to trade it off when the timing is right. Once you know the reason you believe a certain asset is worth trading into, ask yourself what's your ultimate goal is. What do you expect out of this trade? Then take what you expect and formulate a positive exit strategy. Once your asset reaches the point you set forth as the profit target, get out of the trade. Sure, there are some exceptions to this rule, such as when you see a large change in market reaction or liquidity. In your early days as a trader, though, I believe it's best to have a hard set of rules. Flexibility can come with experience.

The inverse of the positive exit strategy is the negative exit strategy. Unfortunately, we are not Nostradamus and we will all make mistakes in the trading world. One of the keys to being a successful trader is to minimize these losses when we are wrong. In my opinion, it is absolutely necessary to have a stop loss GET OUT NOW!!! number. Once an asset goes down to that predefined number, we sell. No matter how much we wish we were right or think we might be right in the future. If the market changes back towards the positive we can always buy back. Many times, we can buy cheaper than we sold for.

Emotions try to play such a large part in trading, yet it should play almost no part. One way to handcuff your emotion and keep it out of the way is to have these predefined exit strategies. Although I believe you always must have some flexibility with your positive exit strategy, I'm a firm believer in a rock-solid negative exit strategy. Don't trust yourself when you're losing money. Greed when going up is certainly powerful but it pales in comparison to the power of fear on the way down. You will always just want to get back to "even." That is the recipe for disaster. Since many exchanges have stop-loss orders and limit orders, your exit strategies can be fully automated. An easy way to look at this and remember it is the following: Prior proper planning prevents poor performance. Remember to look before you leap, think before you act and strategize before you trade.

Wrapping It Up

The world of trading can be murky water full of sharks and shipwrecks. Nevertheless, it can also be extremely profitable and fun to boot. Before you just jump into these murky waters, make sure you dive in the kiddie pool and do more research first. Then maybe wade into the shallow end. Eventually, you'll be swimming in the deep. Okay, okay enough with the water analogies. In all seriousness, though, most people should probably stay away from the trading game. It is a game that can be conquered only with mental effort and discipline. If you don't think this game is for you, it doesn't make you weak. It simply shows that you can recognize your strengths.

If, however, the idea of trading strikes a chord deep in your gut, go for it full force. Begin your journey now. Become a learning machine and soak in all there is to know. Book knowledge can only get you so far, though. True learning comes from the experience. So, put your nose to the grindstone and go make some money!

PRO TIP: Remember, time has a cost associated to it. Make sure you're spending your time wisely and make sure you understand the time cost. More money can always be made, but time can never be earned back. Crypto day trading can be a very time-consuming process if you don't do it the right way. If you make good money but all you do is sit in front of your computer screen staring at it 15 hours a day, is it really worth it?

Chapter 4
Cracking Investing

Investing is defined as committing capital to a business, person or property with the expectation of a return higher than the original input. The key word there is "committing". Unlike trading, investment requires a much higher level of commitment. Commitment to an idea. Commitment to a project. In the world of trading, you are thinking about sentiment and how to make a quick buck off of a particular crypto asset.

To truly commit funds to long-term investment, however, you have to dig deep into each project and technology. I want to give you some important things to look for in a crypto asset before you invest in it. Additionally, I want to give you some basic investment strategies that can allow you to take that knowledge and properly utilize it inside the marketplace.

Now, you may be thinking to yourself, "I don't have enough money to get into investment." In traditional forms of investing such as stocks and bonds and mutual funds, you would probably be correct. This is none of that though. There are endless opportunities to invest at a very small level and potentially turn it into something big. Just think about Bitcoin 6 years ago or Ethereum 3 years ago. There is no traditional investment market to compare the crypto market to. That being said, if you're going to catch the next big coin while it still costs under a dollar, it's probably not going to happen by random chance. After all, there are hundreds of so-called altcoins out there. Many of them trading for under a cent much less under a dollar. Most of them will be worthless in two years. If you want to pick a needle out of a haystack, you need to get a metal detector. To become a successful investor, build a mental toolbox or, pardon the lame analogy, a "crypto detector." These tools are built through research, time and effort. You must invest wisely! A crypto asset or coin could go completely belly up… or, at the very least, go way down in value for a long period of time. This research ability is critical to your success.

Before we begin the research process, however, the first thing we need to do is develop an investment objective. Your investment objective will help you determine what kind of crypto assets you will be looking for. In order to make this process simple, I have included a few questions below to help you determine your direction ahead.

- What is your ultimate goal in this investment? (Don't be modest or extravagant. just be honest.)
- How long do you envision staying fully committed to this investment? AKA, when would you ideally be looking to withdraw?
- How much fluctuation can you tolerate in the value of your investment?
- What is your current level of knowledge in the crypto asset investment world?

As you can imagine, these questions will help determine what kind of volatility we will be targeting.

For example, if you have a good risk tolerance and your goal is to make $1,000,000 in 2 years or less, you will want to set yourself up with an aggressive portfolio designed to have a high upside, along with the risk. If, however, your biggest concern is day to day financial freedom and less stress, you may want to look at something that will have modest, yet consistent, returns.

I break down your overall options for crypto asset investment into three basic categories.

1. The top five. (Based on market cap and liquidity, these are the "safest bets." In the world of crypto, though, there is no true safe bet. It is still too new and too volatile to have a sure thing.)
2. Mid-range established altcoins. (These are coins that everybody in the crypto community are aware of. You should be able to find multiple sources of information both for and against.)
3. Initial and early coin offerings. (These are the new kids on the block. Very little is known about them other than what they want to tell you. There may be some diamonds hidden here, but much of it will just be the rough.)

Once you put together a good investment plan, it is time to

start looking and researching some investment options. No matter which of the three crypto asset categories you lean more towards, each one should be heavily investigated and analyzed fundamentally. Now, let's break down what you are looking for in each potential investment option.

Asset Type

Most newcomers to the crypto community look at all crypto assets as cryptocurrency. This is simply not the case. In the trading world, we can look at every coin in a similar fashion due to the short-term view that we would have. Our ultimate goal in trading is simply to buy low and sell high. The type of asset you are buying is not important beyond whether or not the value will go up in the short-term. In investing, however, your asset type becomes exponentially more important. All coins are most certainly not made alike.

Asset Type 1: Currency & Store of Value

This will be the most familiar asset to you as this is the type Bitcoin represents. This type is really where the crypto community got its start. The characteristics of a crypto asset that is meant to be a currency or store of value are quite simple: It must represent a medium of exchange, a unit of account and a store of value. If all three of these characteristics are met, then it can truly be called a crypto "currency". Major cryptocurrency examples that fall into this asset class include Bitcoin, Bitcoin Cash, Litecoin, Dashcoin, and Dogecoin, among others. The ultimate goal and the public backing of these coins are for the simple reason of having a decentralized option for the storage and spending of money.

Asset Type 2: Utility

A crypto asset that functions as a utility is one that has future value and provides access to a specific product or service. These tokens will derive long-term value from the value of the product or service they provide access to. If the product or service takes off in a big way, then obviously the demand for the tokens necessary to access set product or service will also take off. one of the more well-known and obvious examples of Utility crypto asset is filecoin who raised 257 million in an initial coin offering the provided access to their file storage and sharing service.

Asset Type 3: Security

Security assets had become a new hotbed topic within the crypto community due to the regulations that designating a crypto asset as a security brings along with it. The truth is that you will find crypto assets that function as securities no claim to have some form of utility. This is done to avoid any regulation; however, you will need to become astute at recognizing the difference. Eventually, regulated security coins will probably become extremely common with the ability to buy Tokens that represent shares of Company stock. For now, you will have to determine if there's any actual value to an unregulated security asset that has no future utility or currency aspects. Again, these are the things that don't matter nearly as much in trading but matter greatly in a long-term hold investment strategy.

Asset Type 4: Computing

Computing cryptos provide a platform for financial applications to be built on. Obvious examples of these include Ethereum and EOS. The innovations, such as smart contracts, that have come out of these asset types will likely change the way the entire world economy operates over time.

Researching Your Assets

Now, with a basic understanding of different types of crypto assets, let's look at a few critical aspects we should be researching about each asset before entering a long-term investment.

Purpose

One of the most important questions you must ask is what is the purpose of the project the cryptocurrency represents?

Regardless of whether the asset we choose is a security, a utility or a currency, we are not investing in the coin, per se, but in the project behind it. For currency coins, you're looking at distribution, whether it is store of value or meant to be a daily spendable currency, etc. For a utility or security asset, you will be looking at long-term scalability, potential public demand, and generally whether you believe in the product or service behind the asset. I always ask myself, "what hole does this company fill in the marketplace?" What problem does it solve? Is it just a cool sounding idea, or does it solve a real-world problem? Again, remember that these are important questions to ask no matter what category of crypto you're looking at. Some coins out there that look to be worth a significant amount now will eventually crash and burn because there's nothing solid behind them.

As the world of cryptocurrency evolves, many coin offerings will be trying to sell an idea that solves the same problem. While the base idea may be very solid and have a great need in the marketplace, usually only one or two will prevail in meeting this need. Be smart enough and informed enough to realize the difference between solving the same problem and solving a similar problem. take Facebook for example. Facebook and Myspace could not both survive and thrive in the same market. Although Myspace was the early, more established technology, Facebook prevailed. In contrast, Twitter, Pinterest, and Snapchat Are all other versions of social networks. They are all able to survive in a similar market. The difference between these and Myspace's collapse is that Myspace was meeting the same need whereas Twitter, Pinterest and Snapchat have all attacked similar but different needs. Learn to recognize the same sorts of situations within crypto.

When you do find multiple currencies looking to solve the same problem (for instance "fast transactions and less confirmation time") you have to ask yourself what makes one better than the other. What makes one the best? This involves researching both your coin and the competition. Virtually every crypto offering out there has a white paper that you can find on their website. This will outline exactly what the crypto is attempting to accomplish or fund. Spend some time on their website take a look around. Does it look professional and high-quality? If these guys are as good as their white paper says they are, they should be able to build a solid website fairly easily. Remember that all white papers are written with obvious, extreme bias by the company that's promoting the crypto. Learn to distinguish between the facts and the hype. The good news is, even if the crypto you are looking into isn't the best option you will likely find out which one is, so you can invest in that one.

Community Consensus

Once you have found your MVP candidate, it's time to dig

into the nitty-gritty details. It's time to hop around all of the crypto discussion boards on Reddit and Steemit. No matter how truly amazing any cryptocurrency is, it will have plenty of detractors on those discussion boards. Keep this in mind when looking at the negatives. Look for consensus. If you see consensus across multiple boards about certain efficiencies or deficiencies in a currency, you may want to take those seriously. One of the most serious deficiencies to look at is any security issues that discussion boards are talking about. You may not be an MIT cryptographer that can see every flaw inside each crypto's coding, but I bet you can find a few on the forums. Because of the nature and purpose of many in the crypto community, there is an overall willingness to help each other. Just as a side note, if you're going to ask others to contribute to your research make sure you give back and post information you find out on that thread.

Supply

One of the most overlooked aspects in the public's valuation of certain cryptocurrencies Is its maximum supply. Take Bitcoin for example. Bitcoin has a maximum supply of 21 million coins. That means after the final Bitcoin is mined, there will never be another. This relatively small limit is one of the main reasons the price of Bitcoin flew to insane heights in 2017. Anytime you have a more limited supply of something, then the classic rules of supply and demand come into play. Think of the US Treasury. They continue to print money for years and years and years, increasing the total supply to astronomical levels. This is one reason why $0.10 used to buy you a burger that now costs $5.00… classic inflation. The more money you print or, in our case, the more coin you supply, the less the value of each unit is.

Just because a coin is trading for a low dollar amount does not mean it has the potential to get to a Bitcoin level. Even if everything went perfectly right, look at the total market cap. Look for coins trading for only a few dollars or less but still in the top echelon of market cap. These are the coins with a very high supply. Though the supply may still be limited, it can be in the billions instead of the 21 million limit that Bitcoin has. It is economics 101. If the supply is far too high, then the demand will never rise to meet it. This doesn't mean that coins like that won't survive if they have good utility. Just don't expect them to be trading in the thousands anytime soon.

If a currency has an extremely high supply, then demand can only raise the price so much. Once the initial excitement or surge ends, if the supply is tremendously greater than the demand, the asset will have nothing to hold its value up. Be very cautious and make sure you do your research on any asset that has no cap. There are certainly projects out there that are very solid and have no cap. From what I've seen and what I know, however, those are the exception to the rule for now.

Distribution and Availability to Purchase

the distribution of a coin takes place through proper marketing and agreements with exchanges. If a coin is not distributed on a large exchange or multiple exchanges, it can lead to a lack of volume. distribution and availability. These details must be looked at from two different perspectives. If it is an early-stage project or ICO, early lack of distribution can present an amazing opportunity for an investor. If the coin is not readily available or well-known, yet the project behind it is solid, you may be able to buy into the early stages of something that will expand quickly upon proper distribution. From the other angle, however, you must realize that no matter how extraordinary the project is, distribution must be achieved.

When you come across a scenario such as this, you must look deeper into the project and find out what their long-term plan for distribution is. If they are showing a lack of planning or initiative in that area, personally, I always will stay away.

Marketing

Marketing has always been at the core of a successful business model. In the world of crypto assets and ICO's, this still rings true. As the world of crypto continues to expand, marketing will become even more important. As I look into a new asset, I look to see what their target audience is and how they are reaching that audience currently. I also investigate what their future marketing plans are. Remember that the marketing of any crypto asset can be extremely misleading. Many times, I'll find that the claims they make are outrageous once I look into their technology.

Decision

Once you've done your due diligence, it is time to select the crypto you're going to invest in. As I have already made clear, I am a huge proponent of not putting all your eggs in one basket. I strive to find a few assets that I can stick with long-term. Even if one of them is a big winner, it would overcome the others not moving or moving negatively.

Just as there is a mental game to be played in trading, there are also psychological aspects to investing. You must balance the ability to hold on to your investment through extremely volatile times. You may see your investment drop by 50% or more and still need to hold it. On the flip side, however, you will need to use your knowledge and judgment to understand when it's time to cut your losses. This is a very difficult and delicate balance to find. Go into an investment with an exit strategy, but make sure it is not too extreme one way or the other.

If I am investing in a well-established crypto asset that has a very wide base such as Bitcoin or Ethereum, I am much more tolerant of wide swings. Why? Because the trend continues to go up regardless of the occasional downswings. If I am holding a newer crypto asset, however, I'm a little more cautious to try to avoid large falls in price. This is due to the lack of history and knowledge of whether it will recover from a large fall. Volatility is a well-known aspect of crypto assets; nevertheless, there is obviously such a thing as too much volatility in a downward direction.

Research and learn to understand trends. Be able to look at the chart from a long-term perspective and assess whether current market conditions are causing negative volatility. one thing to clearly look for is when an app set is moving against the swelling tide. if you see a string of days where an asset is losing while the bulk of other assets are winning, it could be time to reassess your investment. Be flexible in your Investments but not frantic in them. Be stubborn but not stupid. Do your research, learn the market, and make sound decisions. You won't always be right, but you will win out in the long run with good, sound investment strategy.

Investment Strategies

Dollar Cost Averaging

The dollar cost averaging strategy has been a staple of investment strategies in the stock market for quite some time. In many ways, I believe it fits the cryptocurrency markets even better due to the volatility. Dollar cost averaging is meant to cut your total investment up into small, bite-sized pieces bought at regular intervals. This reduces risk by allowing investments to be made over a wider period of time and over a wider span of price points. It also lends itself very well to savings plan investments where one puts a specific portion of their salary into investments upon receiving a paycheck. When the market is as bullish as the cryptocurrency market was in 2017, there is an obvious ROI disadvantage compared to lump sum investments. When it comes to investing, you are not looking for the quick dollar, though. You are looking for the long-term, safer bet. Balancing risk and safer bets. This is a massive strength of the dollar cost averaging strategy.

Heavyweight

The heavyweight strategy is meant to put more of a financial focus on your more stable assets. To put more weight with the heavyweights as it were. For strategies such as this, I would put a large percentage, such as 50 to 60%, of my assets into what I believe are solid, top 5 crypto assets. An additional 20 to 30% would be placed in mid-range, well-established assets. The final 10 to 20% would be placed in more speculative and new assets such as initial coin offerings and "penny cryptos". Strategies such as this balance out your portfolio and provide more long-term stability. Included with the stability are still large upsides on the smaller portions of your investment.

Rebalancing

Rebalancing is a strategy that has been recommended by investors and financial advisors for decades. Just as the above strategy is meant to balance your portfolio, the rebalancing strategy does exactly what it says. A rebalancing strategy takes a portfolio and constantly evaluates and rebalances it based on recent market moves. For instance, if I were using the above strategy and had 10 to 20% of my Investment Portfolio in speculative assets and one of them jumped in price by 200%, my portfolio would then technically become unbalanced. In this scenario, after I get done with my victory dance, the rebalancing strategy would demand that I sell a portion of the investment that matured and then use that portion to purchase more medium to low-risk assets. By continuing to do this, over time you will maintain lower risk while being sure to cash out on large gains before risking losing those gains due to unforeseen circumstances.

To the Moon

Throughout the crypto community, you will hear the term "To the Moon" quite often. It denotes the idea that a low-cost crypto (usually an ICO or penny crypto) is going to take off like a rocket to the moon and you're going to ride it all the way there. The running joke is that most investors ride the rocket till it's about a hundred feet off the ground then jump off and take their profits. Obviously, if you got into Bitcoin in 2013 and bought a few hundred Bitcoins, you are now a millionaire. There are certainly cases such as the Winklevoss twins who amassed close to a billion dollars because they bought in early on Bitcoin and held. The obvious issue with this strategy is that 99% of the time you are not going to get 200x or even 2x on your investment. Most of today's ICOs and penny cryptos will likely be long gone in 5 years.

Used alone, this is an imbalanced strategy that has high risk but obviously very high potential reward. If you have a very small amount to invest and don't wish to continue investing, perhaps you could take a shot on a crypto asset that you truly believe in. As I have said many times, an investor must always be prepared to lose their entire investment in a worst-case scenario. you should never invest money you cannot afford to lose no matter what the strategy. In this type of strategy, however, where you are investing on an unproven and unknown ICO or penny crypto, you should not only be prepared to lose your investment, but you should probably expect to. You only have to be right one time, however. I have never been much of a gambler if I can avoid it. I'm certainly not afraid of risk, I just don't like to expand risk to unnecessary levels.

Spray and Pray

What I refer to as the "spray and pray", is just another expanded form of the above strategy. Meant to give you more of a chance of getting on that "rocket to the moon", it involves spreading your investment across many penny cryptos as opposed to placing all your bets on one or one small group. The theory is that if you placed 50 "bets" on small cryptos, and one of them returned 100 to 200 x you obviously would make a large profit. While, in some ways, this is more balanced than the above strategy (which is not saying much at all), it is certainly not the safest strategy. The one thing that I would say is that if I were to ever do something like this I would never just throw my money into something I don't understand or know about. You should never take the lazy way out and just "spray and pray" to get lucky. If you just want to get lucky, go down to the local casino and try the craps table. If you're willing to do the research, however, spreading your investments over several low-cost, high-upside assets certainly has the potential for a great ROI. Again, you just have to be prepared for the inherent risk of losing all or most of your investment.

Value Investing

Value investing is an advanced strategy that requires a knowledge of the entire market as well as multiple assets within that market. A value investor is constantly looking for assets that are undervalued due to recent public sentiment or lack of knowledge concerning the asset. Value investing is all based around intrinsic value. As opposed to market value, intrinsic value is the value that you, as an investor and researcher, put on a particular asset. As a value investor, you are betting against the crowd. Essentially saying that you know more than the public market. Value investing is how Warren Buffett amassed much of his fortune. Throughout his life, he is made a few extremely well-informed and well-timed purchases of companies that were highly undervalued. In much the same way, one can find highly undervalued crypto assets. Because of the immature nature of the crypto market as well as the constant influx of brand new crypto investors, there will definitely be opportunities with undervalued assets. That being said, however, you must set yourself apart from the crowd by doing what they are not willing to do. You must immerse yourself in the crypto Community as well as keep up with the behind-the-scenes activity on multiple assets. This is the only way you will be prepared to make an informed decision when the opportunity arises.

Wrapping It Up

I'm a strong believer in the investing side of crypto. It has made me a lot of money over time. In fact, crypto investing has made many people millionaires over the last few years and I believe it will make many more over the next several. That being said, I want to reiterate again how important it is for you to do your own research and find your own strategies. Again, I am not a financial advisor, nor should you follow mine or anyone else's including a financial advisor's advice without doing plenty of your own research. You obviously have the initiative in the drive to learn more or else you wouldn't be reading this book in the first place. Go out, dig in and learn more.

Chapter 5
Cracking Mining and Staking

Thus far, we have covered some basics on trading and investing with individual cryptos. Now it's time to dig in a little deeper and learn some about how income can be generated through the underlying technology. Crypto mining and staking can be massively profitable if done correctly. What many newcomers sometimes do not understand, though, is that it can also be a time waster and a money loser if you are not careful. The concept behind mining and staking can be somewhat confusing unless you understand blockchain technology. If you haven't read it or want a quick refresher, go back to chapter one and go over the section on blockchain before we dive in.

Now, as we have already said, the blockchain attempts to take out the middleman in a financial transaction. In order to do this, there can be no central authority monitoring the transactional ledger. The idea of a distributed, open ledger was created specifically to facilitate the decentralization and removal of the middleman. This is referred to as a "trustless and distributed consensus". Each blockchain has a series of computers connected to the network and given access to view the ledger and append it upon network consensus. Each of these computers are generally referred to as a "node".

To make it easier for the general public to have viewing access, online tools called block explorers have been created. Each crypto transfer or transaction has an associated transaction ID called a "TxID". From a block explorer, you just enter the TxID number and you have direct access to see the wallet of the sender and the receiver. So, in the example above, person B can look to see that Person A's wallet did have enough money to send the specified amount and that he has sent that amount. Person A can also look to see that person B did, in fact, receive the amount he sent.

Although open visibility, in and of itself, is great, it is not a solution to keeping the ledger error-free. Most people would not want to have to verify each transaction themselves and, even more important than that, if one transaction is verified incorrectly by an individual, then all the following transactions would be incorrect. Much like a checkbook, the ledger would be unbalanced and would throw off everything in a domino effect.

For all these reasons there is a validation necessary in the distribution of the ledger. In order to provide a truly trustworthy validation of transactions, consensus is needed. This means that multiple validations must take place from separate validators that then form a consensus that the transaction is, indeed, real. In order to get a large network of validators, persons across the globe are given incentive to validate and confirm as many transactions as possible. When person A sends money to person B, the transaction is broadcast throughout the entire blockchain network. Validators across the network then go to work to verify the transaction is legitimate. Once a transaction block is sent to the validators to be verified, there is a "arms race" of sorts to see which node can properly validate the transaction and add it to the ledger first. The winner of this race receives a monetary reward in the crypto asset that they are validating a transaction in. This incentivized validation is based around a set of hard rules that must be met in addition to accuracy and speed. By incentivizing accuracy and speed and requiring validators to follow a defined set of rules, it eliminates potential errors while still expanding the validation network due to the monetary incentive.

Blockchain Protocols

Within the world of blockchain, there are different protocols. Bitcoin itself is a protocol and that protocol produces the coin. Ethereum is another protocol. Litecoin is yet another and the list goes on.

Within the different protocols of blockchain, there are different formats of validation. The most common validation (and the validation used by the original crypto, Bitcoin) is the proof of work validation.

Proof of work uses mining as its validation procedure. Crypto mining requires an extensive computer calculation to be performed to add a new group of transactions (a block) on the blockchain ledger. Mining serves two purposes at the same time: 1. It verifies and validates transactions to avoid any double spending of crypto assets. 2. It creates new coins or tokens for the given asset.

The validation of the transaction itself through the open ledger is, in fact, simple; however, in the proof of work system, to receive the first-place reward, there is more to it than just adding up the numbers and verifying that person "A" has enough money to send to person "B" in this transaction. After the financial numbers are verified, the validator must then solve a complex mathematical problem using computing power to find the random "key" that unlocks this block transaction. This mathematical puzzle uses asymmetry and it's designed to be difficult to solve while, at the same time, easy to verify that the solution is correct once found. The first validator to solve the computational puzzle gets a financial reward.

Because of the complexities of finding this key, hundreds if not thousands of verifications of the actual financial details happen before the key is ever solved. After solving the key, that key is broadcast along with the transaction throughout the entire blockchain network. Once it has been broadcast is officially added to the ledger on each and every node, where it will stay permanently.

As a recap, the base principle of crypto asset mining is the idea of block rewards. A block is a group of transactions that have taken place within the blockchain. As a new block with multiple transactions comes out, it needs to be solved and confirmed. Each block has a cryptographic hashing algorithm that functions as a key to placing that block officially on the blockchain. Bitcoin miners everywhere run advanced computing systems to try and solve that algorithm key. The first miner to solve it receives a set amount of the asset being mined.

Mining Pools

Contrary to some YouTube videos you may watch out there, mining is not as simple as flipping on your computer and downloading a mining app. Because crypto asset mining has become such a profitable venture, it inevitably attracted large organizations who wanted to get their piece of the action. This, combined with the meteoric rise in popularity of crypto assets, has led to a more difficult process to run a profitable mining operation. In today's environment, to mine Bitcoin profitably would take a massive upfront investment on equipment. We will get more into types of equipment you will need shortly;

however, suffice it to say that the level of equipment needed to profitably mine on your own would be very expensive.

As it became more and more apparent that average people could not run a successful mining operation on their own, mining pools were formed to gather dozens, hundreds or even thousands of people together in one large mining pool. Each miner within the pool is given a percentage of the overall pool's profit based on that user's computation power and contribution to the overall mining effort.

You will find as you look around that there are many mining pools to choose from. Always be aware and careful of a group's reputation when choosing a mining pool. I would highly recommend using one that has an established track record with plenty of reviews across Reddit and Steemit. In the world of online finance, you simply cannot be too careful. You need to make sure you are researching properly anyone that you decide to do business with. This becomes even more true for a situation like the mining pool where you will be trusting someone else to take payment for your services and divvy them out equally to you and the other miners in the pool. As with everything else we've mentioned in this book be sure to do your due diligence and research on anything you decide to move forward with.

Mining Equipment

As we mentioned above, large enterprises have massively expanded mining operations throughout the world. As time has gone on, technology has risen to meet demands within the mining market. In today's mining environment, rarely will just a standard CPU be profitable to utilize in mining. Because of this, other ideas and equipment have sprung up to fill the gap. Think of it this way… during the Gold Rush of the 1800s, those who truly found success or the ones that were looking in the right location based on research they had done. No matter how much gold there was in California, you still had to look in the right place. The way you look in the "right place" in crypto mining is to use the proper equipment. If you are not using proper equipment the chances of you finding "gold" are minuscule to none.

There are two main types of equipment that are used by individual miners in 2018: GPU and ASIC miners.

GPU Miners

GPU stands for graphics processing unit. A GPU is an electronic circuit designed to speed up the creation of images being output to a computer display or monitor. All computers have chips that render images to monitors, but a GPU is a highly premium model to a normal graphics chip. The GPU is a powerful computer in and of itself. Initially, they were created to assist with 3D Graphics that have since been applied to a myriad of other uses. This is due to their enhanced, focused ability to repeat the same task over and over at an extremely efficient rate. This trait is what makes them so effective as a crypto mining unit.

While all GPUs are powerful, they are certainly not created equal. certain GPUs mine different coins better than others. For this reason, it is important to decide which crypto assets you will primarily be mining before you purchase a GPU. As with anything technological, the landscape of which GPU to buy for which currency is an ever-changing one.

In any case, one of the great advantages of GPUs over ASIC miners is their ability to mine any of the mineable crypto assets. This gives users the flexibility to switch between crypto assets and mine the asset that is most profitable at that time. This can change based on several factors including the price of the asset and how many other miners are currently actively mining. Calculators are available online to measure the profitability of certain coins along with the cost of running a certain GPUs or ASICs. There are even platforms that function is a mining pool they will automatically switch from crypto asset to crypto asset, mining only the most profitable assets.

Building a GPU mining rig can be somewhat complex, but it can be learned. I'm not going to go into the nitty-gritty details about constructing the rig, however, if you would like to construct your own rig and need some direction and doing so, there is a ton of info online. Unlike an ASIC miner, GPUs are not manufactured for the purpose of mining. this means you will want your GPU Miner to be built to specifications that will satisfy the primary purpose of mining. The same thing goes if you have a mining rig built for you or, more commonly, buy a prebuilt GPU mining rig. Check out the mining resources tab for some direction on where to look.

Perhaps the absolute most important thing to consider when building your rig should be overall up time. Every second that your mining rig is not working is money lost. This means there should be several backups automatically built up to avoid single points of failure.

Many serious miners have backup equipment ready to replace inside their GPU Miner. Even if you buy a pre-built one it is wise to have some backup equipment for CPU elements which are more likely to fail. Examples of this include the motherboard and the power supply unit. Obviously, the GPU unit itself would probably not be a great backup. If you had the most expensive portion of the GPU mining rig just sitting around you would probably want to build a whole new rig to double your mining capability. Again, just remember that if your equipment is down you are losing money that you will never be able to recover.

Mining rigs naturally have a lifespan due to the changing nature of equipment and the fact that it becomes exponentially harder to mine a coin the older it becomes.

ASIC Miners

ASIC miners have some amazing pros over GPU Miners and, conversely, also have some severe disadvantages. ASIC efficiency is extremely high in comparison to a GPU unit. The cost of operating an ASIC is still expensive but much less so in a comparable GPU. Because ASICs are built only to mine a specific coin, they will mine that specific coin much more efficiently, quickly and powerfully than their GPU counterpart. The flip side of that bitcoin (pun obviously intended), however, is the fact that you are limited to only mining one coin. Also, it would only take a change in the hashing algorithm for that coin to render your ASIC completely useless. When an ASIC is rendered useless, either by changes in that hashing algorithm or, more commonly, by becoming outdated and unprofitable, the resale value is very small in comparison to a GPU which has other uses outside of mining. In the short-term, there is no question that ASIC miners have a greater short-term earning rate. It is just a matter of whether you can maintain that high level of ROI for long enough to be a better choice than a GPU Miner.

Because of the small number of manufacturers of ASIC

units and the high demand for them, particularly due to the increase in interest in cryptocurrency in 2017, there have been shortages of available ASIC units. Following basic supply and demand, this leads to inflated pricing and high cost of entry.

If you are going to go with an ASIC Miner, be sure to do all the research necessary and always attempt to get the newest technology out there. Don't try to save a few hundred dollars only to find out that your ASIC is obsolete after using it for 2 months. Spend a little extra and give yourself the maximum amount of usage. The common theme running throughout the book is here yet again... Do your research!

ROI Calculation

As we have already noted, like many other business ventures, mining will require an upfront investment to purchase the proper equipment. In addition to the initial equipment cost, you must also look at operating costs.

Operating costs are comprised of Electrical expenses and maintenance of equipment. Do not take these costs for granted. Especially the electrical costs. Electrical cost can literally wipe out your entire profit. If you think I'm kidding consider this, the newest models of ASIC miners consume as much monthly power as the average American household. GPU mining setups also use extensive amounts of power.

Due to the constant operation cost and the initial equipment cost, it is extremely important that you calculate your Roi before entering a mining endeavor. To calculate the ROI, you must calculate what your expected daily mining income will be. This can be accomplished by taking the hashing power of your GPU or ASIC and calculating your gross profit by looking at the mining difficulty of your chosen crypto asset. once the gross profit is no and you can subtract the operating cost in Hardware cost to find your true net profit and ROI. Sound a bit complicated for your taste? I don't blame you. Thankfully, this potentially complicated Roi calculation has been simplified for you using mining calculators you can find online.

One final thing to consider… As we saw in the first half of 2018, crypto can be a wild ride of ups and downs. With these ups and downs, comes severe changes in profitability. The down swings can also be times of incredible opportunity.

Some larger organizations or mining pools may greatly reduce or even eliminate their mining operations for certain coins. With this, comes an increase in profitability and more likelihood of success. Mining equipment is also starting to be more economically attainable due to the now decreased demand. As with every other subject in this book, there are always new and fresh opportunities to make money. You just have to pivot with the market.

PRO TIP: Before we go any further, I would be remiss not to warn you that there are some real potential disadvantages of holding your own mining equipment. Beyond the incredible cost of operating the high-end computing machines, there is the very real problem of noise and heat created by these units. Large mining rigs, whether ASIC or GPU, can put off immense amounts of heat. Some miners literally use it to heat their entire house during the winter. In addition to the heat output, the sound of the units is a real issue. You will want to have a place set aside that has both ventilation and can be closed off to avoid the noise. These are all things to consider before diving in headfirst. If all of this is a real turn off to you, it's probably time to talk about Cloud mining.

Cloud Mining Contracts

If you love the idea of Bitcoin mining but don't want to have to deal with all the research and gathering all the technical knowledge needed to purchase, build and run mining equipment, there are options for you. cloud mining, otherwise known as cloud hashing, allows customers to buy or rent mining capacity. Crypto mining data centers exist all over the world now. Some major companies have decided to rent out their computing power. With this option, all mining is done "in the cloud".

The advantages to this option are obvious. No equipment to set up and maintain, no space to house the units, and no concern with the excess heat that units give off. Obviously, you also will not be directly paying for electricity cost involved, but the cost incurred by the mining company will certainly be passed on to you in your fee structure. The fact that you do not own the mining equipment means that you do not have to deal with it once it is obsolete. Obviously, it also means that you will not have any resale value.

Before we go any further with cloud mining, there is a big warning that I must give you. Because of the nature of it, it can be very hard to verify whether or not a mining company truly exists. What do I mean by that? There have been and will continue to be plenty of scams out there that claim to have lots of mining equipment, give you great rates and promise great things. Unfortunately, these scams have absolutely no equipment and are simply there to trick you out of sending some cryptocurrency to them which you will never see again. This begs the question of how you can tell the difference between a scam and the real deal. In my opinion, the most obvious way is to look at their track record. If they've been around for a long time and been paying out consistently, chances are they are going to stay legitimate. As with anything in the crypto Community or in the world in general nothing is ever guaranteed. As we've said before the crypto community sticks close together. Be sure to check out reviews of your mining company on Steemit and Reddit. There will certainly be people with hidden agendas, but the overall consensus should tell you whether the company is one to be trusted or not. Time to cue the broken record: DO YOUR RESEARCH!!!

Depending on the cost of electricity in your area combined with the time investment it will take to do things yourself, in some cases, cloud mining can be more profitable than doing it the old-fashioned way. More cases than not, however, your profit will be less as, obviously, the mining company will be taking a significant cut for their own profit. In the end, you will just have to weigh the advantages and disadvantages and decide which way to go

Mining contracts can last anywhere from days to years. Understand that the longer the contract the less predictable your profits are. This is due to the increasing difficulty of predicting crypto mining networks, crypto volatility, technological advances and the fact that a crystal ball has still not yet been invented. I personally would highly suggest going with contracts that don't last longer than a few months. A few months is an eternity in the world of crypto. If you don't believe me look at any stretch of months in the wild 2017 or the first half of 2018. Not just in price swings but in all the events and changes that occurred.

Proof of Stake Verification

There are numerous attempted alternatives to proof of work verification, but none have shown more promise or been more widely adopted then proof of stake verification. That being said, there are very few use cases on a large scale. At its current stage and state, from a money-making standpoint, I am not that impressed.

So why am I including it in the book you may ask? One word. Ethereum. Ethereum has been planning for quite some time now to move from proof of work to proof of stake or at the very least a hybrid of the two. There are many within the community that doubt this will ever happen and there are plenty of others that are certain it will happen very soon. If and when it does happen, such a large use case will likely prompt a number of established crypto assets to also attempt to move in addition to new crypto assets coming out as proof of stake coins. For this reason, I think it is well worth it to learn about proof of stake and potentially even take a look at investing in some of the current proof of stake coins.

While proof of work verification was the foundational

verification process in cryptocurrency, there has been a push recently four major cryptocurrencies to move to a completely different kind of verification protocol called proof of stake. There are already cryptocurrencies and assets using this verification process with some top cryptos considering moving to it in the near future. Other cryptocurrencies have talked about moving to a hybrid system where both validation systems are used. In my opinion, the two primary advantages of proof of work are energy efficiency (the proof of work verification process consumes gigantic portions of energy as we discussed some above) and less risk of centralization (no massive mining conglomerates). As the crypto market expanded so rapidly in 2017, increased calls for an alternative arose. Proof of stake as an idea has been around for quite some time but it is gained enormous traction due to these recent changes.

So, what is proof of stake and how is it different from proof of work? As indicated by the name, proof of stake requires the validator to maintain a certain amount of ownership of the cryptocurrency they will be validating transactions in. Most crypto assets that have decided to use proof of stake have released all their coins prior to transactional trading. This means that there are no block rewards as there are no more new coins being created. The validator has the transaction fees as their sole source of reward. For this reason, instead of being referred to as "miners" proof of stake validators are generally referred to as forgers. Not as in forgery the white-collar crime, but as in the shaping of metal. I personally am not a big fan of this term simply because of the explanation I just had to give you. Due to the fact that I hate that term and since I am, after all, the author, I'm going to use my "creative license" here to attempt to "forge" a new term. For the purpose of this writing, I will refer to validators within a proof of stake system as "stakeholders". Bloody brilliant, I know!

As we said, in order to validate transactions and place new blocks on the blockchain ledger, a stakeholder must stake their own money via coins within the network they are validating in. In theory, this means they are incentivized to validate the correct transactions as they have a stake in the overall health of the asset.

Obviously, as you can imagine there are potentially ways to game that system. In any distributed consensus you must protect the integrity of the system and the asset. There cannot be any loopholes or ways to game the system. There are multiple strategies that claim to completely avoid a scenario where a stakeholder could take advantage of the system. One such strategy that is already in use and expected to be used by Ethereum, involves implementing circumstances under which a bad validator might lose their deposit completely. If the validator violates a set of hard rules, they would lose their entire stake. As long as the minimum stakes are large enough, this would make it impractical and unprofitable to attempt to manipulate the system in any way.

Now that you understand some basics about what proof of stake is, let's talk about how to make some money from it. In order to become a stakeholder or forger of a specific crypto asset, you will need to research the requirements for that particular asset. Each asset's requirements are so different that putting a tutorial of any kind in this book would be a waste of space. As with researching crypto assets for investing, your research can be done by looking at the asset's website and checking out Steemit.com, Reddit.com, and Github.com. Once your research is complete and you have implemented the necessary resources and programs to delegate your coins as a stake, you will officially be in the running to validate transactions.

So how are you chosen? Obviously, a network will have multiple forgers validating transactions at any given time. For proof of stake to work, there must be a method for choosing which stakeholder will be the next validator. as you can imagine, selecting only the largest stakeholders would create a very top-heavy environment. You know, the kind where the rich just keep getting richer and richer. Believe me, on its surface it doesn't sound all that bad once you are one of the rich ones. nevertheless, we have all seen systems that were far too unfairly advantageous to those who had money while holding down all those who could not reach those heights. For this reason, programmers have come up with methods that try to counteract this. Two of the main methods used currently are "randomized block selection" and "coin age-based selection"

Randomized block selection selects users at random but still gives heavier weight based on the size of their stake and the size of their hashing power.

The coin age-based selection process gives heavy weight

to the age of the coin or how long a particular forger has held his stake. There is a minimum number of days (generally 30 in most use cases) before coins must be held before a stakeholder can compete for a block. from there, once the stakeholder is selected and validates the block, the coin age of that stakeholder is reset to zero upon which they must wait an additional 30 days in order to be considered again. This provides a fair environment that does not give so much weight to extremely aged coins or holders with the largest stake. Not to mention, it incentivizes stakeholders to keep holding as they know approximately how far away they are from their validation and fee reward.

In addition to the transaction fee that you will gain upon being selected to validate a block, most crypto assets that use proof of stake offer a target interest rate which stakeholders can look to earn. For those of you looking to become long-term investors in certain assets, I would highly recommend that you look more into additional strategies such as staking. This strategy literally puts your money to work for you. As with anything in investing there is plenty of risk involved. In the worst-case scenario, should a coin lose most of its value and not recover you would also lose most of your investment.

Obviously, this is not just a set it and forget it strategy. As with all the investing concepts that were covered in the investment section, you must stay informed and on top of the information and rumors concerning your asset of choice.

CLOSING

In so many ways, we have touched only a little bit on a lot. It is time to move forward with what interests you. Don't try to do it all. I know I am being a bit repetitive here, but repetition is truly the mother of all learning. Focus your efforts and skills on one thing at a time. Do your own research and come to your own conclusions. Remember to always find good sources of information. Sift out the misinformation from media outlets that have no clue. Once you find your good sources, trust them… but verify the information. Never be too lazy to do your own work.

Always remember that this is not a short game. Get in it for the long hall and do everything with that as the end goal. You will have failures. Some you will find could have been avoided and others not. Regardless, learn from them! The only bad failure is the one you learn nothing from.

Lastly… Just freakin go jump in and crack it!